To Saul,                    Sydney, Australia
                                May 1978.
Lots of love on
your 11th Birthday
from your Auntie Sue,
Uncle John & Cousin Katie.
      (Sorry its so late)

The Aboriginal
Children's History
of Australia

Carol Maralngurra, Oenpelli, Northern Territory

# The Aboriginal Children's History of Australia

Written and Illustrated
by Australia's Aboriginal Children

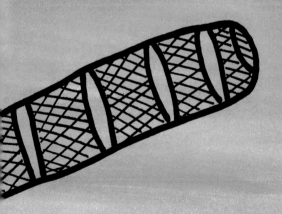

**Rigby Limited**
Produced in association with
Island Heritage Limited, Hawaii
with the assistance of the
Aboriginal Arts Board of the
Australia Council

National Library of Australia/Cataloguing-In-Publication Entry

The Aboriginal Children's History of Australia

ISBN 0 7270 0236 8

I.  Australia — History — Pictorial Works
II.  Children's — Art — Australia

759.994

Rigby Limited ● Adelaide ● Sydney
Melbourne ● Brisbane ● Perth
First Published 1977
Copyright © Aboriginal Arts Board, Australia Council
All Rights Reserved
Designed and set up in Hawaii by Island Heritage Limited
Printed in Hong Kong by Lee Fung-Asco Printers

# INTRODUCTION

This is a unique book. It is the story of Australia as told and illustrated by the Aboriginal children of Australia.

Through the honest eyes and minds of children, a new vision of Australia is unfolded—the Australia of the Dreamtime. The time when the Ancestors of my people emerged from the eternal sleep beneath the surface of the land and created the mountains and rivers, the deserts and forests which form the landscape; the Australia of "before-the-white-man" when we lived in harmony with nature, on our traditional lands; the Australia of the missions and cattle stations, as we tried to come to terms with the newcomers whose arrival had rapidly changed our lives; and the Australia of yesterday and today, when Aboriginal children are growing up in the country, cities, towns, and settlements in a world that is very different from that of their grandfathers. They are going to school, and learning and playing just like other Australian children, but they are conscious of being Aboriginal. They are the inheritors of a rich cultural past that lives on today and that determines the way they see and think about the happenings around them.

It is the element of surprise and joy in what the children see that makes this book unique. Through the natural simplicity of their words and paintings, they convey their enjoyment and enthusiasm for the land which has been theirs for over 40,000 years.

The story of Australia revealed in this book reflects the poetry and imagination of the children who tell it.

It speaks in a language that will be understood by children and adults throughout the world.

For us, the older generation of Aboriginals, it is important that our children have had this opportunity to express themselves. They have been able to turn back to their past, to listen to the stories and memories of the old people, and to make them a part of their own lives. But at the same time they have spoken directly from their own experience. This book reflects their feelings about what life is like today and what it might be in the future.

The Aboriginal Arts Board is proud to have sponsored this project. Since its inception, the Board has worked to foster a sense of cultural identity amongst Aboriginal people. This book has awakened Aboriginal children throughout the country to an awareness of this identity and a pride in their past.

Many people have assisted in producing this book. I would especially like to express appreciation to the many hundreds of children who contributed stories and paintings. Unfortunately, not all the work contributed could be included. Particular thanks are due to the teachers who made this project a part of their school activities. To the many others who helped in different ways, including members of the staff of the Aboriginal Arts Board, I would also like to say thank you.

Through the efforts of all these people the Aboriginal children of Australia have been able to tell their story and give to everyone the opportunity to see Australia through their eyes.

Wandjuk Marika
Chairman
*Aboriginal Arts Board*

# LIST OF STORY-TELLERS

Acknowledgments to artists are given beneath
the individual paintings and drawings

Leo Janbin Albert, Wattie Creek
Adrian Ariuu, Daly River
Ruth Nangala Armstrong, Wattie Creek
Monty Banjo, Daly River
Teddy Barkly, Weipa
Barratja, Yirrkala
Kathleen Barrgibarr, Galiwinku
Patricia Boka, Maryvale
Kenny Brown, Bathurst Island
Lucia Carlingun, Daly River
Roy Chevathen, Weipa
Noel Cooper, Maningrida
Margaret Cullens, Amoonguna
Gerald Darcy, Maningrida
Elizah Dennis, Roper River
Alan Jungarai Dickson, Yuendumu
Edward Dingul, Roper River
Timothy Jabada Donald, Wattie Creek
Jack Jabanangga Donnelly, Yuendumu
Willie Dundamen, Mornington Island
Elsie Edimintja, Docker River
Darryn Fernando, Bathurst Island
Edwin Fernando, Bathurst Island
Karen Foster, Alice Springs
Tony Gabalanga, Maningrida
Stanley Jangala Gallacher, Yuendumu
Jimmy Nayjali Ganambarr, Milingimbi
Leon Garlett, Perth
Gaye Goongonia, Mornington Island
Paul Yawundjurr Gumana, Yirrkala
James Bayung Gumbula, Galiwinku
Ted Marrawili Gundara, Galiwinku
Jeffrey Humphries, Perth
Adrian Intalui, Bathurst Island
Jabangardi James, Warrabri
John Jimarun, Port Keats
Mary Joseph, Areyonga
Philip Jungarai, Yuendumu
Renee Junmulumburr, Maningrida
Kaye Mary Kantilla, Bathurst Island
Patrick Kantilla, Bathurst Island
Dominica Katjirr, Daly River
Geraldine Kerinaiua, Bathurst Island
Gerard Kerinaiua, Bathurst Island

Billy Jangala King, Wattie Creek
Jerry Jangala King, Wattie Creek
Amy Kunarai, Areyonga
Irene Lama Lama, Maningrida
Jimmy Jabanangga Langdon, Yuendumu
Tim Jabangadi Langdon, Yuendumu
Bobby Larking, Port Lincoln
Joe Lynch, Cape Barren Island
Michael Lyons, La Perouse
Billy Magala, Bamaga
Maureen Maloney, Daly River
Robert Mansell, Cape Barren Island
Stephanie Mansell, Cape Barren Island
Patricia Marfua, Daly River
Gary Waninya Marika, Yirrkala
Beverley Napanangka Marshall, Yuendumu
Andrew Nungarrayi Martin, Yuendumu
Cecilia Martin, Daly River
Brian Maru, Mowanjum
Dianna Merrkiyawuy, Yirrkala
Billy Miller, Port Lincoln
Graham Miller, Perth
Alice Mongari, Yirrkala
Kevin Julama Moroney, Wattie Creek
Hamilton Japaljari Morrison, Yuendumu
Pauline Mrilmin, Yirrkala
Francis Damien Munkanomi, Bathurst Island
Ancilla Munkara, Bathurst Island
Angelo Munkara, Bathurst Island
Berchman Munkara, Bathurst Island
Michael Munkara, Bathurst Island
Bobby Manganbuy Munumggurr, Yirrkala
David Marputja Munumggurr, Yirrkala
Margaret Nabananga, Wattie Creek
Audrey Nagamara, Wattie Creek
Annunciata Namida, Daly River
Shane Namurki, Maningrida
Susan Nangala, Wattie Creek
Thecla Nayeri, Daly River
Angela Neidacowie, Daly River
Fergus Ngakyunwokka, Aurukun
Tony Ngakyunwokka, Aurukun
Pamela Ngallametta, Aurukun
Stephen Ngerdu, Mowanjum
Fay Nungarai, Wattie Creek
Dorothy Nurra, Daly River

Melva Pahimbung, Aurukun
Joachim Papajna, Bathurst Island
Martina Parry, Daly River
Mark Jabangadi Patterson, Wattie Creek
Hal Janama Peanut, Wattie Creek
Loma Peter, Weipa
Joyce Petner, Mount Isa
Arthur Poantimillui, Bathurst Island
Neville Pootchemunka, Aurukun
Clement Portamini, Bathurst Island
Guy Pungura, Yirrkala
Francis Xavier Puruntatameri, Bathurst Island
Theresa Puruntatameri, Bathurst Island
Jacob Raburabu, Goulburn Island
Johnson Janama Ray, Wattie Creek
Matthew Jagamara Raymond, Banka Banka
Billy Jabangadi Robbo, Wattie Creek
Jimmy Roughsey, Mornington Island
Mandy Roughsey, Mornington Island
Marlene Sarmardin, Mount Isa
Doreen Spratt, Alice Springs
Finton Timeapatua, Bathurst Island
Barnabas Tipiloura, Bathurst Island
Connell Tipiloura, Bathurst Island
Cosmas Tipiloura, Bathurst Island
Jonathan Tipungwuti, Bathurst Island
Les Tjifisha, Daly River
Jimmy Pitjara Toby, Lake Nash
Maurice Umbagai, Mowanjum
Denis Daymbalipu Wanambi, Yirrkala
Mayawurr Wanambi, Yirrkala
George Djiliwuy Warrawibi, Yirrkala
Christopher Wells, Launceston
Douglas Wilson, Yuendumu
Elvira Wolmby, Aurukun
Sarah Wolmby, Aurukun
Susan Wolmby, Aurukun
Alison Wukutjpa, Yirrkala
Reggie Wurjal, Maningrida
Cynthia Yunkaporta, Aurukun
Iris Yunkaporta, Aurukun
Brian Gaymuniny Yunupingu, Yirrkala
David Malati Yunupingu, Yirrkala
Jimmy Dyipu Yunupingu, Yirrkala
Kathy Dela Yunupingu, Yirrkala
Rosemary Daylulu Yunupingu, Yirrkala

# Contents

# I. DREAMING

The sea rushed to touch the shore; along the shore stood white hills, they were sacred hills, for this was the land where our two Creators landed.

Along the edge of the water two figures moved closer and closer spearing fish. They were called Djankawu and Barama. They divided the Yolngu (Aboriginal people) into two groups which they called "Dhuwa", which Djankawu was, and "Yirritja" which Barama was.

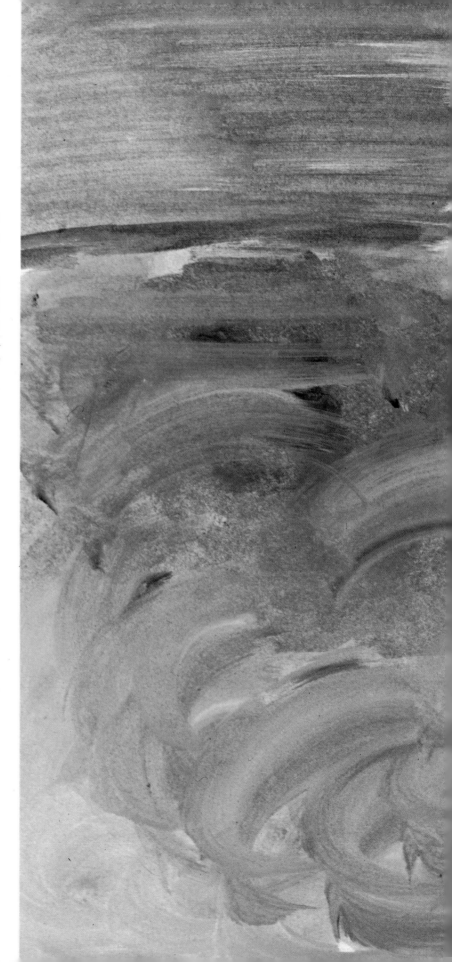

*Dianna Merrkiyawuy, Yirrkala, Northern Territory*

This was way back, at the very beginning. The land and the people were created by the Spirits. They made the rivers, the water holes, the hills and the rocks and all the things living. They gave us hunting things, they gave each clan their land, they gave us our totems and they gave us our Dreaming.

*Carolyn Windy, Docker River, Northern Territory*

First of all there was no light and the world was full of darkness. It was so dark that people, animals or birds could not see. They had to stay in one place.

One day all the animals gathered together and said "Where can we get light?" They talked and talked about this but nothing happened. Finally the Frog said that he would make the sun come up by singing his magic song. So he began to sing. He sang and sang. He was singing for a light to clear the darkness away.

Marshall Jabangadi Poulson, Yuendumu, Northern Territory

Maureen Maloney, Daly River, Northern Territor

Suddenly, there behind the hills, the sun was making its way across the sky, shining brightly on everything. Every living thing was happy. They all went from place to place because they could see everything around them, trees, grass, hills, and rivers.

*Roy Chevathen, Weipa, Queensland*

*Susan Tjutjana Inkatji, Ernabella, South Australia* 15

Everything was full of life and happiness.

In our tribe Wandjina made the whole world, birds, trees, rocks, animals, people, you and me. He gave us the land divided equal and gave us totems to look after. He punished us when we made mistakes. He is said to be our grandfather's God before we were born, and those with and before him.

*David Tipaumantimirri, Bathurst Island, Northern Territory*

Maurice Umbagai, Mowanjum, Western Australia

Wandjina is important.

The only things left that carry us back to Wandjina time are the paintings on the caves and stories of the old people.

When you see his face, different shades of colour represent different forms of clouds in many kinds of weather. White is the cloud, yellow is the distant cloud in the afternoon, red is the cloud filled with lightning, black is the raincloud. His heart is in the centre, but he has no mouth and we do not know why, it is a mystery to us, beyond our understanding.

*Andrew Jorda, Mowanjum, Western Australia*
19

Our old people tell us many stories from the Dream-time. Once there lived a great Aboriginal hunter who found a gigantic Brolga with a broken wing. At first the hunter felt frightened and tried to run away, but then he felt sorry for the Brolga so he went up to the Brolga's sad face and asked politely how the wing got broken. The Brolga told the hunter his story and great tears fell from the Brolga's big sad eyes. They fell into the tracks he had made when he was crawling along in pain. The tears were as big as the water of billabongs and they turned into cool fresh water and formed a river flowing very fast down the tracks. While he was telling his story the poor Brolga died of sorrow and woe and the hunter rose into the sky and became the Morning Star. Now he watches over the poor Brolga and only he knows how the great wing of the Brolga was broken, and now we know how the Giddys River was made.

*Dianna Merrkiyawuy, Yirrkala, Northern Territory*                    21

Long ago in the Dreamtime, there lived a young man called Purukupali and his sister Wuriuprenala. Among them lived Wiyayi and her son Jinani. Wiyayi went out hunting and met her lover. Soon Purukupali knew that Wiyayi was always meeting her lover Japara. So Purukupali decided to sharpen his spears and clubs; he was ready to kill Japara. The very next day they fought, while Wuriuprenala hid behind the bushes, and watched every movement of the fight. Purukupali knocked Japara to the ground and lay down his clubs. No sooner had Purukupali laid down his clubs than Wuriuprenala lit a fire beside the dead Japara and brought him back to life. Purukupali gave a small light to Japara, and he gave the biggest firestick to his sister Wuriuprenala. He told them to hold on to the light. Soon Japara changed into the Moon Man and Wuriuprenala changed into the Sun.

Japara gives us the light at night when the Sun Woman Wuriuprenala is asleep. When she wakes she takes her firestick and moves through the sky. At sunset she paints herself red and makes the sky glow red until she falls asleep.

22

*Nanai Maree, Bathurst Island, Northern Territory*

Dominica Katjirr, Daly River, Northern Territory

The animals were really people in the Dreamtime. They changed from being animals to being people like us. We get our totems from this. If we belong to the Brolga totem, then our ancestors were Brolgas back in the Dreamtime.

Long ago there lived a Brolga. She was very proud of her dance. Every night when the other Brolgas were asleep, she used to wander off into the billabongs where there was nobody around. She went everywhere dancing in the moonlight, spreading her beautiful wings. Even today if you go out to our country, the Moil, you will see them dancing close by the billabong where the Bat killed the Rainbow long ago.

*Susan Marrawakamirr, Galiwinku, Northern Territory*

## II. OLD TIME

Before the white men came to our country, our people wandered through the land.

*Lucky Jabaldjari Wclker, Warrabri, Northern Territory*

My grandparents lived out in the bush. They lived in bush shelters and the only work they had was to make their spears and axes from stone while the women had to hunt for crabs, look for food, get the water and mind children. No one had to worry about their clothes as they only wore paper bark.

Sometimes they went out to the hills to paint and draw and sometimes they went out into the bush looking for colours that they used for their painting.

The people had a secret place. It was a cave in the hills in a faraway country. Sometimes the old men went to this cave and they painted pictures on the rocks around the cave. No women or young people were allowed near this cave, only the older men.

*Raphaelia Tipiloura, Bathurst Island, Northern Territory*

*Martina Parry, Daly River, Northern Territory*

The people used to make tools and weapons with stones. An axe is made out of a sharp rock and wood to hold the bottom. A spear is made out of a straight white stick we get in the bush near water lilies. A shelter is made by getting four sticks and putting them in two rows. Two on one side and two on the other. Then we get some bark off the trees, pandanus skin, then paper bark. And there's the shelter.

Our people made bracelets, necklaces, rings and clips to make themselves look pretty. A bracelet is made from shells or stones we find on the beach. A necklace is made out of small cut sticks which are painted. Rings are made out of a circled orange stone and clips are made out of long skinny sticks with curved ends.

They lived a good, happy, rich life. My father told me these things.

*Iris Nuggett Joye, Areyonga, Northern Territory*

31

In the early days on Mornington Island, people used *walpas* or canoes for catching turtle, dugong, fish and other sea food. For shelter they made bark huts and for clothing they wore hair string belts and possum. Fur felt was made from a wallaby skin. The women wore shirts made out of *galna* (or grass). When people got married, the man would grab the woman under her arms and the woman would pretend she didn't want him. The woman got a hiding from her parents and relations if she refused to marry the man.

*Tim Taylor, Walhallow, New South Wales*

*Patrick Mudjana, Maningrida, Northern Territory*

*Lucky Jabaldjari Walker, Warrabri, Northern Territory*

In the daytime the men and women went hunting for food. The men used spears and hunted emus, kangaroos, porcupine, turtles, goannas and rock snakes. They often took their sons with them so that when they grew big they also would know how to go out and hunt the wild life. The women used digging sticks and went digging yams, bush potatoes, and they also found wild plums, and they put all these things in the dilly bag they carried on their shoulders.

*Milton Jabangadi Poulson, Yuendumu, Northern Territory*

The old men taught the young boys how to kill emus and kangaroos and how to find them through the grass.

*Billy Nyapirri Gumana, Yirrkala, Northern Territory*

My relations lived in the bush in their own territory.
Each family hunted and lived in a certain area. Other
families could visit that area, but were not supposed
to hunt there.

Daisybell Marabiakabiakawiar James, Groote Eyelandt, Northern Territory

Gae Mastrosavas, Ceduna, South Australia

Graham Miller, Perth, Western Australia

After the hunting we cook the food. In the old times, we didn't have matches or lighters to make fire, but we had our own idea. The old people would cut two dry sticks, a soft flat one and a hard round one. They put the flat stick on the ground then made a hole in it and put some dry grass in the hole. Then they twist the sticks around and around between their two hands, rubbing hard until smoke comes. They keep going until fire comes and then put it in with the firewood to make the fire.

When they were sitting by the fire they were thinking about dancing and singing and making didgeridus.

Sometimes the older men of the tribe used to tell good stories of the dancing Brolga and the Bat that stole the Rainbow's wives.

Long ago, back in the Dreamtime, there lived a special Bat. The Bat was a very good dancer. All the animals loved to watch the Bat dance. There also lived a Rainbow. The Rainbow didn't like the Bat. He had stolen two of the Bat's wives. They were Whistleducks.

One day, some of the animals wanted to have a corroboree and they invited all the other animals of the bush. The Bat came too and when he saw the Rainbow lying down and the two Whistleducks fanning him, he became very angry. He said to himself, "I will kill Rainbow and bring back my wives."

When the dance ended, all the animals went back to their homes. The Bat also went back to his home. The next morning, he went to a high hill to find a stone to make a spearhead. He did this by cutting his nose to see how sharp the stone was. He tried and tried. At last he found one which he again tried on his nose. This time he cut it right off. It was sharp enough to make a spearhead.

The day of the big corroboree arrived. All the animals came. The Rainbow came. The Whistleducks came, too. The Bat began to dance. He danced on and on until all the animals fell asleep. The Bat pretended to sleep too, until the Rainbow and the Whistleducks were fast asleep. When all was quiet, the Bat jumped up and ran to get his spear from where he had hidden it. He crept up to the Rainbow and speared him. The Rainbow roared with pain and the blood ran down his side. When the animals awoke and saw him rolling over and over, they flew away everywhere. The Bat took his wives back for himself while the Rainbow rolled into the billabong and sank. He lives there now and sometimes when it rains he rises from the billabong and arches his blood-stained body through the sky.

Dorothy Nurra, Daly River, Northern Territory

We have a dance about this story. The dancing and corroboree led the people through their legends. The men and women danced together around the sand and the children ran around the camp fire. Some people liked dancing from morning until night, especially when the moon is shining brightly. Everybody loved these happy times.

*Ancilla Munkara, Bathurst Island, Northern Territory*

Then as the fire died out and all the people were properly tired, they went to sleep. As the fire dies out the children sleep away, dreaming of the legends that were told that night.

## III.  THE MACASSANS

At Drimmie Head there are tamarind trees. They stand tall and strong. They are found all along the coastal areas of Arnhem Land. We call them *Djambang*. The fruit looks like a peanut and tastes like a lemon. We make a cough mixture from its juice. They have lots of branches and small leaves all packed together. They give a great big shade. The forestry men said some of the trees are over 500 years old. The tamarinds came with the Macassans who came from Indonesia with the wind.

48

*Dianna Merrkiyawuy, Yirrkala, Northern Territory*

*Jack Munyarrirr, Ramingining, Northern Territory*

Before the real white people came to Arnhem Land, the Macassans stopped in the river not far from the bay and were suddenly surprised by the Aboriginals, who were standing on the beach with their families. The Macassans were looking for trepang. We call trepang *dariba*. It looks like a black cucumber. You see trepang in the coral when the tide goes out and you just pick it up. You can dive and get it off the sandy bottom too. We helped them to cook the trepang. After it was boiled up, the Macassans used to smoke the trepang in a bush hut. They built a little hut and lit a fire underneath to make it smoky. Then the Macassans went back with the wind and sold the trepang to the Chinese. We called the Macassan people *mangathara*. They looked different to us because their skin was lighter than ours.

They came in big boats we called *Mitjiang*. They were the first boats we had seen and we thought they were big birds floating on the water. They gave our people axes, knives, materials, jewels, pipes, tobacco and grog and took away the trepang and turtle shells. The Aboriginals took the Macassans to hunt for turtle. When they came back from hunting, the Macassans gave some arrak to the Aboriginals and they got drunk and there was trouble. Sometimes people got drunk and fought. Most of the time we were friendly with the Macassans and some of our people went on the big boats to their country.

The Macassans came for hundreds of years. They showed us how to make canoes and they brought money and flags. We fly flags when a person dies to keep people away from the house with the dead body.

Some of our people still know the Macassan language. Many of our words like *rupia* (money), *lipa-lipa* (canoe) and *balanda* (white people) and *ngarali* (tobacco) are Macassan words. At some places we still use the Macassan wells to get our water. There is one on Entrance Island near Maningrida and a special one at Milingimbi.

Shane Namurki, Maningrida, Northern Territory

# IV. THE WHITEFELLAS

### AWAMRIGURR—THE STRANGERS

For many years there were only Aboriginal people living here. They hunted for food and meat for their families. Sometimes they went to the river to spear fish or other creatures in the water.

One day, the men went down to the river to spear the fish. As they came near the river, they saw a boat with some strange men in it. The Aboriginal men were frightened so they hid themselves in the bush, waiting for the boat to come. When the white men came ashore they brought their guns with them. They were standing on the sand talking and they went into the bush.

One of the Aboriginal men went to the top of the hill and stayed there watching the white men come closer and closer. He told his men that the strange men were coming and one by one they took their spears right to the very top of the hill. Then two of the Aboriginals rolled some big rocks down the hill towards the white men. But they saw the rocks coming and hid themselves in a corner. The rocks rolled past them. The Aboriginal men thought that the strange men were killed but they were hiding behind a big rock. Then the white men saw a black man and they fired their gun. The Aboriginals ran away and hid themselves again.

When the white men were finished exploring, they started back for their ship but, as they went past, the Aboriginal men began to throw their spears. The strange men ran and dodged so that the spears would not hit them. They jumped on board their boat and sailed away from the land, and they never came back again. When they were sailing away, the Aboriginal men were standing on the sand watching them. After they had disappeared, the men did a wild dance until it was dark.

*Stanley Jangala Gallacher, Yuendumu, Northern Territory*

## CAPTAIN COOK

Long, long ago Captain Cook sailed to look for a good place to start a little mission. He sailed around the world. He sailed to the nearest place to stop. When he stopped, he saw this place and he knew it was a good place to build a mission. After, he got in a little boat and rowed to the shore. When he got out of the boat he walked towards the beach. He went further and further in the bush. Suddenly a spear came swooping through the bush and nearly got him. So Captain Cook ran back. He was very frightened of us. It was black Aboriginals coming towards him with spears, sharp pointed spears. Then Captain Cook went rowing back to his ship.

*Roy Chevathen, Weipa, Queensland*

## FORT DUNDAS

The British Army went to Fort Dundas in 1824. We didn't kill them because we were friends. There were only 50 of them. But we had 2 000 Tiwis and we didn't worry about their cannons and guns. We were terrific in the bush. The British could catch fish but they were rotten hunters. Our men wore nothing and our women wore bark aprons. The British had black boots up to their knees, white trousers, and red coats and hats. We called them Muruntawi; and that means hot-red faces.

The British came in a boat. There were soldiers, some convicts and marines. They brought buffaloes for work and meat. Some buffaloes ran off and we were happy about the buffaloes because they have big meat.

The British had cannons, guns, axes and all different kinds of things. They had food and they had rum for drinking. The British made bricks from the soil and built a fort. They gave it a name and the name was Fort Dundas.

In the Wet Season they started to have fever, and they were dying, because of wet blankets and they were wearing wet clothes. The convicts caught fever by staying in a small room. Some died and most of them went back to their own land.

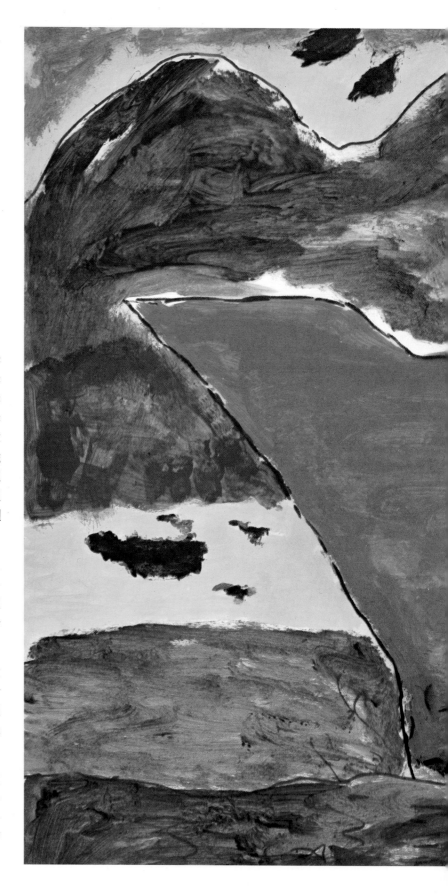

BRITISH SHIP

Connell Tialoura, Bathurst Island, Northern Territory

Today some people go to Garden Point on Melville Island then go to Fort Dundas to see the cannon balls and the walls made of red soil, and the rum bottles that they used to drink out of. Even today, buffaloes are found at Melville Island.

We've always been here but the British stayed for five years. We didn't kill one another but the British captured one of our men named Tambu. He was in a bark canoe and they came in dinghies, tipped his canoe and cracked his head with paddles.

*Kenny Puakilari, Bathurst Island, Northern Territory*

*Alex Ronan, Perth, Western Australia*

## YAGAN

At the beginning when the first white people came, Yagan and his tribe tried to get along with the settlers. Yagan was an Aboriginal hero. He lived near Perth over 100 years ago. In the beginning Yagan had to go out and live alone in the wilderness without any help from anyone. He was very brave and they made special cuts on his back. At first the Aboriginals thought the white men were their spirit ancestors who had come back. Yagan made friends with them but they made war. Yagan talked to Governor Stirling. He told the Governor if the whites killed one of their people they would kill one of the white people. After this some men on a cart shot Yagan's brother. I don't know why, he was just sitting there. This got worse and worse until Yagan and his dad were killed.

The mother cried.

*James Bayung Gumbula, Galiwinku, Northern Territory*

## THE EXPLORERS

There was a European man called John MacDouall Stuart. He decided to go to Darwin. He had big troubles with the Aboriginals; he had troubles with food too. It was very hot. They had two camels. They walked and walked and walked.

*Howard Jungarai Wayne, Yuendumu, Northern Territory*

In the old days when the explorers and prospectors were travelling around here, the local people, the Walbiris, didn't know white fellas. Some white fellas used to travel through Walbiri country while others used to turn back frightened. Some of the whites would give the Aboriginals food and tobacco, but at this time they didn't know what sugar and tea were. When the white fellas gave them food and other things, the Aboriginals said they were being kind and they would let the whites pass through their country. They said they were to be left alone; they weren't to be killed. They thought also that the whites were some sort of spirits, some of the Walbiris said, "Let's kill them because they must be devils or evil spirits." But the old people here said, "Leave them alone!" And these whites were able to continue on to Western Australia. Some other whites came through this place and some of the Walbiris said, "Here they are again—the same ones back again."

When these people saw a white traveller on horseback for the first time, they thought it was a single being and they only saw the difference when the fella got off his horse. The people said to themselves that these must be some kind of spirits or monsters. Only a few of the people knew about whites and they told the others that those creatures were just horses—they were just ordinary animals like the kangaroos.

Another lot of whites turned up after with camels this time. Two unarmed Walbiri men went up to them and made friends with them. The whites asked where to find water, and gave tobacco to the men. Then they showed the whites to water. They met up with another group of Walbiri people camped at a water hole. These people picked out two more guides for the whites and they led them to the next water hole where another pair of guides was found.

*Johnothan Jagamara Ross, Amoonguna, Northern Territory* 67

The original guides would then return to their group. The Walbiri people led the white fellas from water hole to water hole until they reached another people's country such as Waringarri and Walmajarri. No Walbiri would go near those people's country as these were the Walbiri's worst enemies.

The white fellas who came through this country used to carve their names on tree trunks or on rocky hillsides. There are lots of these marks around.

In about 1928, when these people (whites) came through here with my uncle as their guide and interpreter, they came across one of the last lot of wild people who had never seen a white man. They were wild but they would just show them the water holes and let them go through their country. The whites didn't interfere with the Walbiri women because the women used to run away frightened and hide in the bush.

At that time Yuendumu settlement didn't exist. It was in country belonging to the Anmajiri people— the country more to the west belonged to the Walbiris. The Walbiris and the Anmajiris didn't go into each other's countries. The Walbiris would always bypass the Anmajiri country and keep well to the west. Only my uncle travelled through both countries as a guide to the explorers and prospectors.

When a bore was sunk in Yuendumu, people other than Anmajiris started going there.

*Linda Clyne, Amoonguna, Northern Territory*

## CONISTON

In 1928 a group of Aboriginals was working for a white man. The white man was sleeping with an Aboriginal wife. Then he took one woman for three days and told the men he would shoot them if they didn't leave him alone. The old men made an arrangement so they could kill the white man. The old men asked the woman to shout out so all the men ran to where the white man was sleeping. They threw boomerangs at him. Then old Japanangka cut his throat with an axe. Then the old men dragged the white man to a rabbit hole, and pushed him inside. After that they went to another place. Another white man went to visit the white man and discovered what had happened. He quickly went off and got the police.

*Mary Joseph, Areyonga, Northern Territory*

The white men rounded up a mob. They started looking for the killers. The white men saw some Aboriginals in a camp. They surrounded them in a circle and shot every one of them. The killers were running away but the white blokes shot other Aboriginals.

But Japahangka and Japaljarri were too tricky. They hid themselves in long, thick grass. The white men still kept on following. They had an Aboriginal tracker. They saw a mob of Aboriginals at a water-hole. They were camping. They shot them.

Matthew Jagamara Raymond, Banka Banka, Northern Territory

Mary Joseph, Areyonga, Northern Territory

*Emmanuel Kurungaiyi, Port Keats, Northern Territory*

# NEMARLUK

Nemarluk was a Murinbata man from Port Keats country. He was a tall strong man and had four wives and he was a really good hunter. He didn't have a rifle. He had a *damul* (spear) and a *dunbit* (spear thrower).

Before the war some Japanese came to a beach in our country. They were looking for fish. Nemarluk didn't like white people or Japanese. They shot our people and stole our women. Nemarluk wanted to kill the Japanese and take their boat. He told the Japanese he would help them hunt some ducks. When they were in the bush his friend Kumaiyi hit the Japanese over the head with a club. Then Kindari took the Japanese man's gun and shot him. Nemarluk and Mainmair killed the other Japanese on the boat with axes. Some Tiwi Aboriginals from Melville Island who were on the boat as crew ran away to Darwin.

Police came out with horses and dogs to catch Nemarluk but they couldn't catch him for a long time. When they did catch Nemarluk and the other men, they chained them up and took them to Darwin gaol. But they couldn't keep Nemarluk there. He jumped over the wall and swam across Darwin harbour and escaped to his country.

The police and Aboriginal trackers chased after him and they had a man from the Malak-Malak tribe called Bulbul to help them. Nemarluk and two of his wives kept away from the police for years. They ran and walked while all the police had horses. Sometimes he followed behind the police.

One day Nemarluk was camped near Legune Station and Bulbul and another tracker pretended to be stockmen. They sneaked into Nemarluk's camp and cracked him on the head. Nemarluk had blood in his eyes and couldn't see. Bulbul put chains on him and then they made him walk to Darwin which was hundreds of miles away.

Nemarluk was in gaol for a few years but then he got sorry for his country and got sick and died. It was during the war with the Japanese.

## TASMANIA

Once upon a time there were some Aboriginals. They lived in Tasmania.

Then white men came to live in the Aboriginals' land. They took over the land and treated the Aboriginals very badly. The Aboriginals were killed. Those who were left fought back and the white men got lots of soldiers and made the "black line." The soldiers were a short distance apart and they marched across Tasmania hunting the Aboriginals in the bush but the soldiers could not keep track of them.

Then a man called George Robinson came and took the Aboriginals to Flinders Island. They were put in houses and they were given pots, pans, plates and beds, but they didn't know what they were. They did not like these things. They wanted to go back home but they couldn't. It wasn't long before home sickness and disease caused some deaths. They died because they could not get back to Tasmania. In a very short time there were only a few survivors. These were finally returned to Tasmania where the last to die was Truganinni. Truganinni was the last Tasmanian Aboriginal. She wanted her bones burnt and thrown away in the sea. In 1976 they did it.

*Bobby Larking, Port Lincoln, South Australia*

## THE MISSIONARIES

Long ago, when the Mission wasn't started, there was bush and a lot of jungle. The old Mission place was built on the other side of the river. The old Mission got washed away by the flood. You can still see the old Mission today. It is old and the bricks are falling down.

The white men worked very hard in the old Mission and they built houses for the people. There were five priests and seven brothers and they worked hard in the hot sun. They wore hats to cover their heads from the sun. In the garden they grew rice, tobacco, mangoes, yams, corn, citrus fruit, paw paws. They also had pigs and cattle.

*Dominica Katjirr, Daly River, Northern Territory*     79

Some missionaries wanted to bring children from their parents to look after them. The children lived in dormitories. Their parents were still in the bush. They used to dig up roots and collect berries to bring to the Mission and sell them for flour, tea, sugar and clothes. They learnt new ways and a new language.

The Father and some of them said "Let's stay here" and when all the people came and stayed there, Father taught them about God. Then Father said, "Let's build a big church now that there are a lot of Aboriginal people here."

And so they built a church and he baptised the people. Then he taught them to build houses for themselves and they cleared the thick jungle, and he taught them to grow gardens.

The Mission has grown bigger and bigger. There are many houses in the village. We have a hospital and a school. There are gardens where the people work. There are stock yards for the horses and cattle. There is a good airstrip. Today the people have started their own cattle station and they work very hard out there. They call this land Unia and the children from there come in to board at the Mission and go to school there.

Lillian Banbapuy Ganambarr, Yirrkala, Northern Territory

## THE WAR

The Japanese and Europeans had a big tribal war. They nearly killed Bathurst Island with the bomb.

The Japanese plane came over Bathurst and Melville Islands. The people from Bathurst Island saw the Japanese plane, and ran to the jungle. The Japanese plane threw bombs into Bathurst Island and all the people were frightened. Bishop Gisell sent a message to Darwin and the Australian planes came to fight the enemy. They had a big fight in the sky and two Australian planes got shot down by Japanese planes. One Australian plane crashed on the cliff and one crashed in the jungle. Some Japanese pilots were shot down too.

When Mathias was camping in the bush he saw in the night a white face and black clothes. The Tiwi people knew that the Japanese were hiding on the beach. They rushed to their camp and gathered all their tucker, and billy cans and went off, but a little boy, Clarence, got left behind. His mother and father went back to look for Clarence, but he wasn't there, he had gone with the Japanese. They told Mathias to go and take Clarence off the Japanese. Mathias went to look for the Japanese. He walked and walked. When he found them he hid himself under a bush and waited. Then he saw Clarence. The Japanese were hand carrying Clarence. Mathias waited as they passed, then he sneaked behind them and pulled his revolver from his knee and shouted "Stop." And Mathias said, "Stick 'em up, alasame Hopalong Cassidy!" The Japanese put their hands up and they gave him Clarence back.

*Bunabul, Milingimbi, Northern Territory*

When Hazel was a small girl, she had a sore toe and went to Thursday Island for her toe. Then the war started. The little children were frightened. They were inside the house sitting quietly and the war was coming closer and closer. The soldiers came to Wutan to guard that side area. The submarine started to come in the harbour but the submarine can't come because God put the water shallow. The submarine went back. The submarine tried to go to Weipa but it couldn't get there too. And it went back to its place.

Planes bombed the houses down and people ran to the trenches to hide. So my people used to hide in the bush. The Japanese killed people with guns. The soldiers were at Wutan. The soldiers won the war. And that was all. After the war finished a little baby was born. She was named Peace. That is Aron's mother.

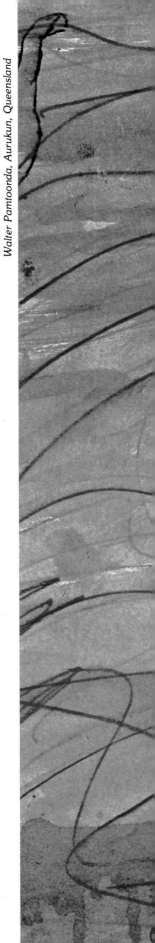

Yiniyalma, Milingimbi, Northern Territory

Linda Clyne, Amoonguna, Northern Territory

## MAPOON

A long time ago the part-Aboriginal children in North Queensland were stolen from their parents and taken by the government men to Mapoon. They were our mothers and fathers and they never saw our grandparents anymore. At Mapoon they were adopted by the tribes people. The Mapoon people were good to everybody. They are very old now. Their houses were made of bark.

Tracey Twaddle, Palm Island, Queensland

*Neville Pootchemunka, Aurukun, Queensland*

Old Mapoon had lots of ducks, geese, fish and some swamp. Some people lived in Mapoon many years ago and they lived there because they liked it. Their houses were near the beach and they got lots of palm coconuts. They had lots of cattle and it was a good hunting place. Their beach was good for fishing. They planted many bananas and other good things. There were many houses and many cattle.

My other grandmother says Mapoon is flowing with milk and honey. That's fine. You can never die in Mapoon because you've got all you want to eat and cure yourself. Mapoon is full of all the things you need.

*Kim Ardler, La Perouse, New South Wales*

## MINING—WEIPA

When they mine bauxite firstly the bulldozer knocks down all of the trees and puts them into heaps. After heaping them, they set them on fire. When the fire has settled, the scraper comes along and scrapes the topsoil away. Then the endloader comes and digs up the bauxite and loads it on to the Haulpak. The bauxite is taken to the bauxite dump and they put it in a "cruncher," then it goes along the conveyor belt to the bene plant where it is washed. Some of it goes to the plant to be "cooked" and turned to powder. The rest from the bene goes by conveyor to the stockpile. It's put onto the conveyor belt again, then loaded on to the bauxite ships. From here it is shipped to different parts of the world.

*Reggie Wurjal, Yirrkala, Northern Territory*

*Ernie Humphries, Nollamara, Western Australia*

*Ben Pascoe, Maningrida, Northern Territory*

## MINING—YIRRKALA

It was at Gove at the place called Nhulunbuy that the white men came and settled down to work. My people thought that it was very bad because they came and pulled down our sacred trees that my father's father used for hunting and dancing place. The Riratjingu and Gomaitj own this country.

Wuyal was the wild honey spirit. He made the mountain at Nhulunbuy and everywhere he went he left sugarbag for the people. The mining people put a water tank on Wuyal's mountain. Our people were very sad and angry.

Before the mining there were animals everywhere and it was a pretty place. Now it's ruined. We've only got a few animals, and there are lots of beer cans and smoke and grog and it's dusty everywhere around Melville Bay. There is a special banyan tree called Dhanburama, right in the middle of the alumina plant. The mining men must not touch the sacred tree because it has the spirit of Wuyal in it. There was a big argument about the sacred tree. There was a big argument about the land. Now white people have to pay royalty money to build houses and the town at Nhulunbuy and to take out the bauxite.

A lot of our people have jobs with the mining. We are friendly with the white people and we play sport with the white kids. Some of our people are drinking grog and it makes them silly. Sometimes they fight. We don't know how long it will take before the bauxite is gone.

*Johnny Mango, Weipa, Queensland*

# MINING—AURUKUN

Now the mining companies want to do mining in the Aurukun area. All the people are not agreed about the mining. Some people from the city come for some meetings. They say "yes" for the mining. Some people said "no" for the mining. Some people said "yes" for the mining.

I would like to work for the mining company and get money for myself, to make a house for me and my family. I would make lots of money and go right around the world to see all the different places. We could travel by car, train, bus and plane so we could see the cities and towns. We could buy some land too. The mining men work day and night. They get lots of money. I wish I could work for the mining company. I would like to drive a Haulpak.

*Carlo Yunkaporta, Aurukun, Queensland*

*Carlo Yunkaporta, Aurukun, Queensland*

*Iris Nuggett Joye, Areyonga, Northern Territory*

## WATTIE CREEK

My grandfather was a stockman at Wave Hill Station. The station belonged to a man called Vestey. He lives in England. He did not pay any money but he gave my grandfather sugar and flour and tea and beef. One day one man and his name was Vincent Lingiari decided to strike, because there wasn't much to eat at that time. He packed up from his job and walked to Daguragu (Wattie Creek). Men and women and children and dogs went with him. They stayed there for a week or two. Then came some of Vestey's men and said to them, "You all must go away from this place." But Vincent said, "You can't get us out of this place. We found it and want to keep this place."

Then a white man came to Daguragu (Wattie Creek) and talked to the Aboriginals. They did not want to go back to the station so they made a house. After that, Vincent Lingiari went to Sydney and Canberra to talk with the white men about the land rights. The Prime Minister gave him back the land. The Prime Minister poured sand on his hand, to show he gave back the land. Now Vincent Lingiari is the owner of Daguragu and Donald Nangiari is the Manager, but it belongs to the Gurindji. Today we are working for our own land with horses and cattle in the stock camp.

*Hal Janama Peanut, Wattie Creek, Northern Territory*

*Leo Janbin Albert, Wattie Creek, Northern Territory*

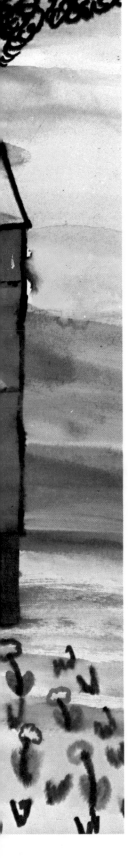

## V. TODAY

Today, Aboriginals have changed. They have a new way of life. A long time ago we did not have roads, but only little paths where the people followed one behind the other. Now roads made by the white men where the big trucks travel are running through our bush lands. The people have changed too. They now have houses made of bricks and iron and no longer paper bark and sticks. Some of our people still go out hunting with spears to kill fish but others go out with guns to shoot kangaroos. Some of the women still go out with their big daughters and they often take their dogs with them, while their husbands are working hard to earn money for their families. Our people are

*Anthony Tipunguuti, Bathurst Island, Northern Territory*

proud because they earn money. Some of the men are driving trucks and tractors and the women are learning new things too. Some are working in the school, the hospital or the office. Children are learning in the school. Life is changing.

They have good clothes which they wear on Sunday when they go to the Church. They know and believe in God. Some others are not Christians yet but it will not be long before they learn all about God. Our Mission is very beautiful.

102

*Johnathan Jagamara Ross, Amoonguna, Northern Territor*

*Joanne Carbine, Port Lincoln, South Australia*

*Andrew Portaminni, Bathurst Island, Northern Territory*

## MY HOME AND WAY OF LIFE

Bathurst Island where I live is a beautiful place. It has lots of coconuts and mangoes and hibiscus trees and frangipanis and bougainvillea and carsara flowers. My house is made of tin and wood. Birthdays, weddings, Christmas and bush holiday time are the happiest times for my family and me and the sad times are when someone belonging to our tribe dies. Everyone is sad and we have special dances and ceremonies. All the dances are called Pukamani. Relations take off their ordinary clothes and paint their bodies and some of the relations put feathers in their hair.

My favourite foods are the food that my people have always eaten. I like white people's food but what I like best is crab, wallaby, mangrove worms, turtle, sugar bag and carpet snake. We catch the crabs and mangrove worms among the mangroves. We cook the crab and turtle usually in water, but the worms we eat just as we get them out of the trees. The best worms are the white ones though the purple and pink ones are good to eat too. The men shoot wallabies with guns now, but before they were killed with spears. Turtles are caught in the sea from a boat but we find the turtle eggs under big mounds of sand on the beach. We cook the eggs in water on the fire. The women make bags for carrying the eggs. These bags are woven from pandanus fibres and the handle is made from vines. My people do carving. The men carve the special sacred poles, to be used at the time of death. One of these poles is placed in front of the house of the dead person and the house is closed sometimes for a year. Then a dance takes place and the Pukamani poles tell us that the dance is for the dead.

*Linda Pupangamirri, Bathurst Island, Northern Territory*

105

In the gulf country the men go out to sea to spear dugong. They look for dugong in the shallow waters where the darm grows. Darm is the seaweed dugong eat. The best time is when the new moon comes up. The nights are dark, the men listen for the dugong blowing its breath. One man stands on the nose of the dinghy with the harpoon in his hands. The second man steers the dinghy with the oar while the third man waits and listens. The dugong has a sharp way of listening too, can hear the sound of its enemies from a long distance.

When the men hear the dugong they cut across to spear it when it comes up the next time. The man with the harpoon throws it at the dugong. He tries to hit the dugong on the back. The barb stays in its back, the harpoon shaft floats to the surface. The first man and the third man hold the rope tightly, while the dugong pulls the dinghy across the water. After a while the dugong gets tired and the men pull it in beside the dinghy and scratch its nose to make it die. They tow it to shore after it dies.

When the men come back with a big dugong we run down to meet them. They cut the dugong up on the beach. First they cut off the tail, then cut straight up the sides and then cut the head off and gut it. They

*Billy Magala, Bamaga, Queensland*

cut the dugong in four pieces and divide the rib bones up.

When it is the prawning season the trawlers come up with big nets and catch them. They bring them into Denham Island and unload them. Then they peel off their heads and pack them into a cardboard box and a plane comes in and takes them away. Some of the parents work there and get pay.

One trawler can get over a ton of prawns. They get two sorts of prawns, banana and tigerprawn. Sometimes the people get prawns to eat, and for bait to catch fish. They catch salmon, queenfish and bream.

The turtle lives in the sea. It eats the grass in the water. It swims fast. When it comes to the top of the water we kill it.

*Willie Dundamen, Mornington Island, Queensland*

Mount Isa is a busy city. People are rushing around all day long. Shops and hotels are always full of people. Jobs are very hard to get. Mount Isa mines are not able to take another person in. The K-Mart has given a few jobs to unemployed people. People who have got jobs had better hang on to them or else. The people of Mount Isa as a whole are alright. Many people are neglected, they are mainly Aboriginals. Many people make fun of them and treat them like dogs not humans. Whites only care about themselves and their family. They never think of how they would feel if they were Aboriginals and were treated that way. Whites should consider other people and how they feel, so should some Aboriginal people who go around "stirring." There is a shortage of houses, most people don't realize this. The Aboriginals in Mount Isa still live a type of tribal life, and they do not mix as well with the outside world.

I go to school in Alice Springs and go back to Elkedra Station for the school holidays. When we get back to Elkedra we go swimming on hot days and we also go fishing, hunting with our grandmother for bush fruits, goannas and other bush food. Sometimes we go walking around the station so our mother can do the washing and cooking. Other times we go and sit under the trees across the creek and play cards or just go to sleep. When it is cold we stay inside our homes and do anything we can find to do. On warm days we go to other places to see our relatives, at Murray Downs, McDonald Downs, Derry Downs, Ammaroo, Utopia and Warrabri. At Elkedra we grow bananas and paw paw trees and citrus trees. My father is the gardener and he grows a lot of vegetables for the station. I like it at Elkedra when we have nothing to do because when jobs are finished my father or my uncle takes us out to get kangaroos and turkey around the station.

Graham Kelly, Lake Nash, Northern Territory

Today our men use saddles on their horses when they muster the cattle at the Moil. Sometimes a big transport truck with three trailers behind it takes the cattle to Katherine in the dry season. Sometimes the stockmen have a rodeo in the yard. If the horses are wild, they put them in the other yard and break them in. During the wet season all the horses and cattle are put into yards. The men work very hard at the Moil. This is their own country and their own cattle station.

*Rosemary Nungarai Morris, Libanungu, Northern Territory*

*Robert Simpson, Alice Springs, Northern Territory*

I was born at Mount Dennison station, and cried day after day. I got sick and my father and my mother and my grandfather and my grandmother took me to the Yuendumu Mission, where the nurses and sister took me to the Alice Springs Hospital. When I got to Alice Springs, I thought the lights were a fire and I thought that the fires belonged to Walbiri people, but when I got closer I was frightened because I saw lots and lots of people who were white and I was scared of these people. And when white people walked by, I would cry.

*Margaret Cullens, Amoonguna, Northern Territory*

The Red Rider is a good skateboard and I am on it.

There are lots of birds. It is quiet in the country. It is better than the city because in the city there are too many cars, trucks, and other traffic. In the country you can go out and feed the ducks, cows, horses and other animals. There are tractors and bikes.

*Richard Timbery, La Perouse, New South Wales*

*Matthew Jagamara Raymond, Banka Banka, Northern Territory*

*Francis Xavier Kolumboot, Port Keats, Northern Territory*

*Carolyn Windy, Docker River, Northern Territory*

I went to the rock 'n' roll dance and I saw one man singing. Some men were drummers and others played steel guitars, and basses and they were making loud noises with their music, and there was smoke going everywhere in the hall.

*Meruya Robuntja, Amoonguna, Northern Territory*

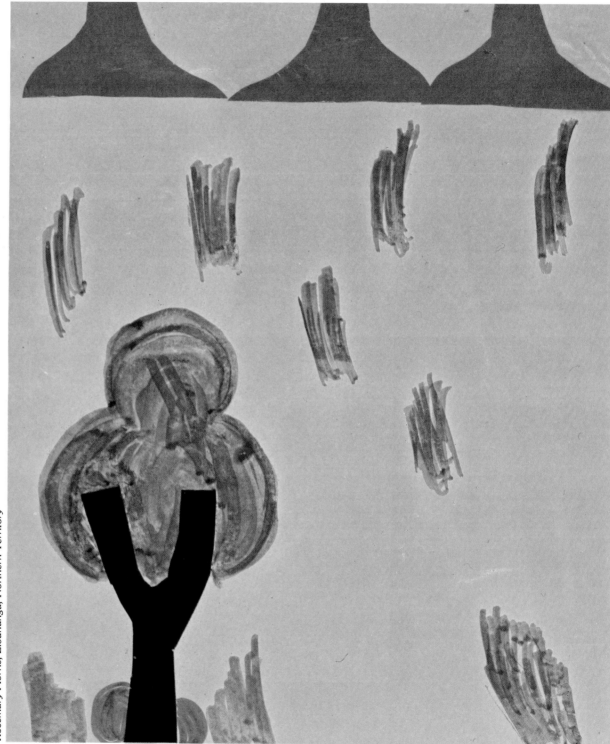

*Rosemary Morris, Libanungu, Northern Territory*

This is my uncle Cyril. He walks around a bit.

This is my uncle Jimmy. He is a stockman. He works at Lake Gregory. He is my father's brother. I have got eight uncles and my young uncle gave me a drive of his brown car, and I was very happy. I have also got lots of aunts at Yuendumu. My uncle likes to play with me, and I like my uncle. I like my old uncle Jimmy and my aunt too. They walk north to look at the country, and lots of water holes round my uncle's country, and they take their boomerang. My uncle likes to go to his country.

I have straight dark brown hair and a little bit of curls. I wear my hair parted on the side. My eyebrows are long and arched. I have dark brown eyes. I've got a wide nose and thick lips.

My uncle lives at Yuendumu. He is young. He is strong and healthy. He can drive a motorbike and he can fix the car and works in the garage. He can drive big trucks. On weekends my uncle goes hunting, shooting rabbits. He can use the gun. He always goes with relations and we always go west road. We camp at the creek and the bore.

*Debbie Miller, Port Lincoln, South Australia*

*Johnathan Bongabonga, Yirrkala, Northern Territory*

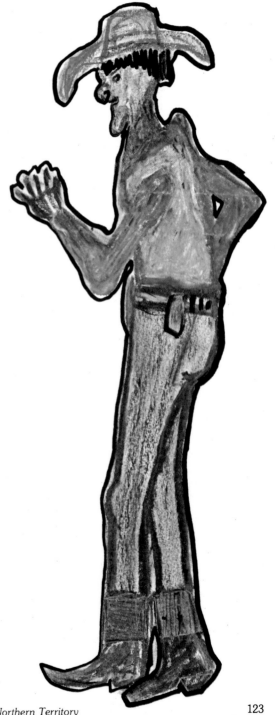

*Ned Jakamarra Wilson, Yuendumu, Northern Territory*

123

# Meet my family.

Joyce Pether, Mt. Isa, Queensland

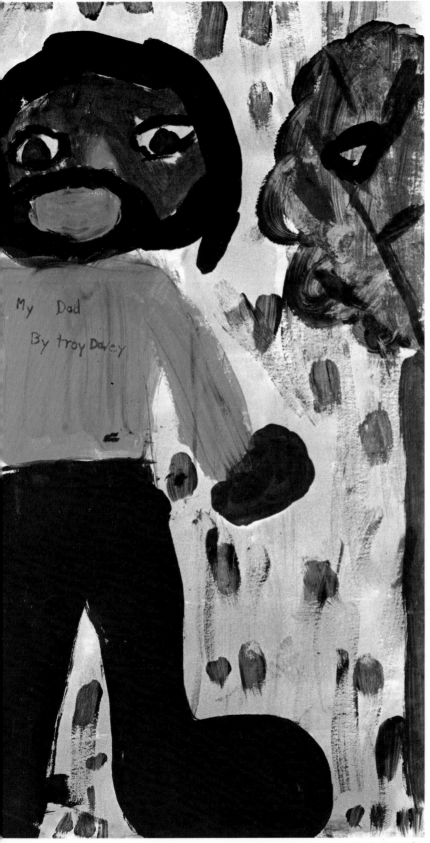

*Troy Davey, Port Lincoln, South Australia*

In my family there are my brothers and sisters, my mother and father. Our place is called Aurukun Mission. My family lives with me. My house is near the main street which runs to the landing. My relatives have meetings and they talk about many places. My times for my family are Saturdays and Sundays. Sad times are Monday to Friday. The special times are dancing at the weekends. Then they eat meat and cakes, have drinks and they wear clean clothes.

I have nine in my family. Inside our home we have cupboards and beds. We put cups and plates inside the cupboard. I live at the end of the house. We plant mango trees around the house and hibiscus flowers. Sometimes our relatives have meetings. We play ball with my relatives. We see our relatives every day. They have meetings if we are in trouble. They talk the right way and show us to do the right thing. The men dance for special times. People eat fish and food and wear clothes at these times. I go hunting with my family. My favourite food is fish and I love to eat fish.

My dad was a boxer. Even today he can knock a man down with his fist. He went all over Australia but he never went out of Australia. He said he would get homesick. He went to Sydney, Adelaide and Brisbane. At home he has a lot of trophies in Queensland.

125

My uncle lived on a Mission when he was a boy. He liked hunting rabbits with a stick. When he left school he worked at the Mission farm but he was drinking and got kicked off the Mission. Then he went to Adelaide and tried to get a job. They knocked him back because he was an Aboriginal. After a few times, he didn't try anymore; he didn't know where to go so he went down to the parklands where the older fellas used to drink. After that he was always drunk and always in trouble. He just used to think about the next flagon. He stole things and went to handout places for food and he spent a lot of time in gaols. Every now and then he'd go bush and go mining or work on farms driving tractors or shearing. Sometimes he picked spuds or went stump picking. He went all over South Australia and Western Aus-

tralia. Once he stopped drinking for a few months and when he was coming back to Adelaide he thought he'd buy a flagon for his brother. But he drank it himself and got back on the grog. After that he drank for a long time and didn't work or even worry about food. He was always down the parklands or in gaol. All his friends were the same. He got real bad and went to a place for drunks. He went back a few times before he stopped but now he doesn't drink anymore. He's trying to stop young Nungas getting on the grog when they come to the cities, and feel lonely and scared. My uncle's 38 and he's been in lots of gaols. Most of his brothers and sisters are dead. Most of his friends are still down in the parklands or dead.

*Maurice Umbagai, Mowanjum, Western Australia*

# MY PEOPLE

*Regina Betts, Port Lincoln, South Australia*

*Regina Betts, Port Lincoln, South Australia*

I think it is a good thing to have an Aboriginal Governor like Sir Douglas Nicholls. I think it is a good idea. We call him the gum-leaf governor of South Australia because he taught some children to play the gum-leaf.

Albert Namatjira is a famous man. He was an artist in the outback. He painted pictures of the mountains and the gum trees.

Once there was a man called Lionel Rose. He was a champion boxer. When he went to other countries he showed them how to fight. Lionel Rose was very good at boxing. Some men were very scared of him. He had a fight with one man called Harada, he said that he was good at boxing. Lionel said to him, "Sir, I will teach you to fight with me. You might be very scared." He then hit him on the nose and that's why Harada looked very frightened.

This is Miss Evonne Goolagong. She is a famous tennis player. Now she is married and is called Mrs. Evonne Cawley. About 400 miles south-west of Sydney is a little town of Barrellan. Evonne Goolagong's family still lives in that town. Her father worked as a shearer on the farm.

*Terry Pascoe, Maningrida, Northern Territory*

*Billy Miller, Port Lincoln, South Australia*

## MY HOMELAND

Cadell River is my homeland. It has a garden. My people grow vegetables and other things. I live at Maningrida too. We have a self-service store, a big restaurant (hasty tasty) and a big town hall. We have gymnastics and films in the town hall. In the restaurant they cook fish, hamburgers, hot chips and chickens. Many people come to Maningrida. Maybe because they like the place. We have a police station.

Maningrida is a settlement. Maningrida is not my homeland. It stands near the mouth of the Liverpool River. In the middle of the mouth of the Liverpool River there is an island called Entrance Island. We often go there for camping or fishing over on that island. That island is really wonderful. Maningrida is a place where both Aboriginals and whites share things, be friends always. My grandmother who is from Blyth River was told by her friend who belongs to the Gunavidji Tribe at Maningrida that long, long ago the Macassans came to Maningrida and stayed on Entrance Island. They came to get trepangs. Aboriginal people at Maningrida work as mechanics, electricians, shop assistants, teaching assistants, nurses, secretaries and other different works but we, the Aboriginals, can still remember the ways of our ancestors.

Some Aboriginals get tired of the noisy transport and miss their homelands a lot. So they go back to their homelands like Kupanga (Blyth River), Gudjanjun-jirra (Cadell River) and follow their ancestors' life.

*      *      *

This is our homeland place called Gurgawuy. We drive there from Yirrkala. It takes a day to get there. We go hunting. We eat turtle and fish. Sometimes the turtle lays its eggs on the beach. We eat the eggs.

When we are back in our own homeland the men make boomerangs and spears and the women go out into the bush and look for pandanus, so that they can make mats out of it, and you can see the women

Lucia Carlingun, Daly River, Northern Territory

making dilly bags and mats. We sell the boomerangs and spears and mats and dilly bags for food and petrol.

\*       \*       \*

Our place is Archer. We live there, my little brother and I, and my father. We live there. That is our place. We like our own place. We like camping, and we like to ride a horse. We were camped out at our place. We cook our damper in the sand. We make our home from ti-tree bark. We hunt for yams, fish, goanna and other food that we can find. The men make spears and woomeras. They hunt for pigs, duck and goanna, and they spear the pig and they carry the pig to their camping place. They cook the pig. They dig a big hole and they put the pig into the hole and they cover it.

We go out for food in the scrub. We dig for yams while the men go hunting for wallaby. Then we come back to our camp. We get some wood. We burn a fire. We wait till the fire is only hot coals. Then we cook our yams. Then we get wood for the wallaby, and some ant bed and bark. We dig a hole. Then we burn the fire in the hole, then we put the ant bed down, then the wallaby. We put the bark on top, then sand.

\*       \*       \*

My homeland centre is at Wulwulwuy. There are four tents there, a big river and some pandanus palms. Whenever we are hot, we go for a swim, sometimes we get cold, then we all run home and sit by the fire. There is fresh water in the river, and many big fish. One of my brothers caught a tortoise and one of my sisters caught a big fish which seemed to have a beard. We often go looking for honey and my mother finds the honey. We chop down the tree and get the honey. When the sun sets we all go home.

We go back to our home country on holidays and other times when we can. It is our land and we can live our way. There are many wallaby and emu and fish and trees. There is no mining at Wulwulwuy.

*Maureen Maloney, Daly River, Northern Territory*

## VI. MY COUNTRY

I love my country. My country is surrounded by sandhills and dry mulga trees and gum trees. In the weekends or holidays the people hunt during the day for bush turkeys, emus, goannas and kangaroos.

The place I come from is dry. Every Saturday we go hunting for bush beans, wild berries, wild tomatoes and sweet tomatoes and potatoes. After we come from hunting we have our supper and I go to play with my friends. Then we go to bed.

*Ned Jakamarra Wilson, Yuendumu, Northern Territory*

This place is on the border near Austral Downs. There are no trees, only yellow grass and no water, and it is very hot. If you go from Camooweal to Lake Nash there are lots of plain goanna and lots of rats. You've got to take some water and plenty of petrol if you are going that way. If your car breaks down, you are finished. The snakes and rats will eat you alive.

In the desert country the sand is very red and dry, and there is no grass. The sun is setting slowly. It is very cold at night and very hot in the day. There are no people living here because there is no water and the creeks are very dry. When the wind blows it brings red dust.

Right: *Iris Nuggett Joye, Areyonga, Northern Territory*

*Johnathan Jagamara Ross, Amoonguna, Northern Territory*

There is a house, but no people are living in it. The water tanks are empty. The only animals living here are the dingoes, the snakes and the lizards.

Right: *Ron Rankin, Tennant Creek, Northern Territory*

I come from a place where there are a lot of sandhills and big water holes. One day we just saw the big red water serpent travelling across the land, with its big red eyes twinkling towards the horizon. He always roams the countryside, especially when it's raining; that's his favourite weather.

The wind blows and brings the rain clouds this way. It brings some water to this dry place. Now the clouds are going to the sea. The sea gives some more water to the clouds. Then the clouds go to another place where it is dry.

*Maxie Japaljarri Davis, Amoonguna, Northern Territory*

140

*Carolyn Windy, Docker River, Northern Territory*

Dorothy Nurra, Daly River, Northern Territory

The sky over the hills is full of colours—yellow, red, pink, white. The trees in the distance look like a man's long shadow. The wide plain has friends—the fence that goes across the land and the trees that stand beside the water hole.

The trees are happy when the wind comes and blows them from side to side, and they dance in time with the wind. When the wind blows gently they fall asleep, but if the wind is rough, they don't like it because it throws away their branches and green leaves.

The birds come and make their nests in the trees. At night everything is very quiet and still. Before the sun rises, the birds awake and with their singing wake up the sun to light up the sky. The kangaroos come out to look for fresh green grass and water, and other little animals are also about. Everyone is glad for the new day.

143

## Giddy's Poem

Listen! What do you hear?
I hear the ripples from the water
The wind flowing through the trees
And the birds in the trees.

What do you smell?
I smell the fresh air around us
The sweet smell of the flowers beyond
And the smell of the lunch being cooked.
I feel hungry already.

What do you see?
I see big shady patches under the trees.
I wish I was sleeping under them.
The trees moving to and fro
No engines or pollution
Just the sound of silence with birds in the trees
And the wind going through the trees.
I would rather live here
Than in a city.

*Marshall Jabangadi Poulson, Yuendumu, Northern Territory*

This is our land. It goes back, a long way back, into the Dreamtime, into the land of our Dreaming.

We made our camp here, and now all that is left of our presence are the ashes and the bones of the dead animals the young men had killed. Soon even our footprints will be carried away by the wind.

# ACKNOWLEDGMENTS

## Schools which contributed material

Alice Springs High School, Alice Springs, N.T.
Dhupuma College, Gove, N.T.
Francis Xavier School, Daly River, N.T.
Kormilda College, Berrima via Darwin, N.T.
Libanungu Group, Wattie Creek, N.T.
Milingimbi School, Milingimbi, N.T.
Port Keats School, Port Keats, N.T.
Oenpelli School, Oenpelli via Darwin, N.T.
St. Therese's School, Bathurst Island, N.T.
Wave Hill Station School, Wave Hill, N.T.
Xavier Boys' School, Bathurst Island, N.T.
Yirara College, Alice Springs, N.T.
Yirrkala School, via Gove, N.T.
Yuendumu School, Yuendumu, via Alice Springs, N.T.
Aurukun State School, Aurukun, Qld.
Bamaga State School, Bamaga, Qld.
Happy Valley State Primary School, Mount Isa, Qld.
Healy State Primary School, Mount Isa, Qld.
Marrilac Hostel, Mount Isa, Qld.
Mornington Island State School, Mornington Island, Qld.
Mount Isa State High School, Mount Isa, Qld.
Palm Island State School, Palm Island, Qld.
St. Michael's School, Palm Island, Qld.
Weipa North State High School, Weipa, Qld.
Aboriginal Community College, Adelaide, S.A.
Ceduna Area School, Ceduna, S.A.
Kirton Point Primary School, Port Lincoln, S.A.
Koonibba Infants' School, Koonibba via Ceduna, S.A.
Mansfield Park Infants' School, Adelaide, S.A.
Port Lincoln South Primary School, Port Lincoln, S.A.
Taperoo High School, Adelaide, S.A.
Taperoo Primary School, Adelaide, S.A.
Yalata School, Yalata, S.A.
Mowanjum Community Group, Mowanjum via Derby, W.A.
Nollamara Primary School, Perth, W.A.
Cabbage Tree Island School, Cabbage Tree Island, N.S.W.
Casino High School, Casino, N.S.W.
Cobar Primary School, Cobar, N.S.W.
Fingal Head Primary School, Tweed Heads, N.S.W.
Guyra Central School, Guyra, N.S.W.
Jervis Bay Aboriginal Cultural Group, Jervis Bay, N.S.W.
Jervis Bay Primary School, Jervis Bay, N.S.W.
La Perouse Primary School, Sydney, N.S.W.
Matraville High School, Sydney, N.S.W.
Tabulam Primary School, Sydney, N.S.W.
Walhallows Primary School, Caroona, N.S.W.
Woodenbong Central School, Woodenbong, N.S.W.
Cape Barren Island Special School, Cape Barren Island, Tas.
Prospect High School, Launceston, Tas.

## For their assistance and cooperation the Aboriginal Arts Board would like to acknowledge also:

Mr Mike Gray
Aboriginal Community College
Adelaide, S.A.

Ms Liz Mater, Ms Celia Aicken and Ms Vivian Rakita
Aboriginal Grants Section
Commonwealth Dept. of Education
Sydney, N.S.W.

Mr J.G. Gallacher
Asst. Director Special Projects
Dept. of Education
Darwin, N.T.

Messrs Colin Young and Denis Schapels
Dept. of Education
Darwin, N.T.

Mr J.H. Barton
Director General of Education
Perth, W.A.

Dr A. Gough
Director General of Education
Hobart, Tas.

Mrs Pauline Leeman
Dhupuma College
Gove, N.T.

Mr Ron Argoon
Yirara College
Alice Springs, N.T.

and all the many other organisations and people who contributed assistance in a variety of invaluable ways.

**A Child's Point of View**
**Library created by**    EDWARD J. McGRATH

**Associate Director**    DYANNE Y.M. McGRATH

EDITORS
Robert B. Goodman
Robert A. Spicer

**Island Heritage Limited**

ASSOCIATE EDITOR
Carol A. Jenkins

ART DIRECTION
Robert B. Goodman

TYPOGRAPHY
Barbara Goodman

The Editors would like to thank
Addressograph Multigraph Pty. Ltd.,
Sydney, for their generous assistance at an
early stage in this project.
A special thanks to Henry and Julia
Strasburger and Pam and Ross Thyer for
their unfailing hospitality.
This book was wholly composed on the
A.M. Compset 500 in Souvenir.